EXPLORING HI-TECH JOBS

Hi-Tech Jobs in SOCIAL MEDIA

Bradley Steffens

San Diego, CA

© 2024 ReferencePoint Press, Inc.
Printed in the United States

For more information, contact:
ReferencePoint Press, Inc.
PO Box 27779
San Diego, CA 92198
www.ReferencePointPress.com

ALL RIGHTS RESERVED.
No part of this work covered by the copyright hereon may be reproduced or used in any form or by any means—graphic, electronic, or mechanical, including photocopying, recording, taping, web distribution, or information storage retrieval systems—without the written permission of the publisher.

LIBRARY OF CONGRESS CATALOGING-IN-PUBLICATION DATA

Names: Steffens, Bradley, 1955- author.
Title: Hi-tech jobs in social media / by Bradley Steffens.
Description: San Diego, CA : ReferencePoint Press, Inc., 2024. | Series: Exploring hi-tech jobs | Includes bibliographical references and index.
Identifiers: LCCN 2023041511 (print) | LCCN 2023041512 (ebook) | ISBN 9781678207106 (library binding) | ISBN 9781678207113 (ebook)
Subjects: LCSH: Social media--Vocational guidance--Juvenile literature. | High technology industries--Vocational guidance--Juvenile literature.
Classification: LCC HM742 .S8337 2024 (print) | LCC HM742 (ebook) | DDC 302.23/1023--dc23/eng/20230905
LC record available at https://lccn.loc.gov/2023041511
LC ebook record available at https://lccn.loc.gov/2023041512

Contents

Introduction: A Popular Activity Generates Jobs	4
Content Creator	7
Social Media Influencer	14
Artificial Intelligence Data Scientist	22
Social Media Manager	29
Mobile App Developer	37
Social Media Intelligence Analyst	45
Source Notes	53
Interview with a Social Media Manager	55
Other Jobs in Social Media	58
Index	59
Picture Credits	63
About the Author	64

Introduction: A Popular Activity Generates Jobs

With 59.9 percent of the world's population—about 4.9 billion people—spending an average of 2 hours and 35 minutes per day on social networking platforms, engaging with social media is one of the most popular pastimes in the world. But today's social media users are seeking more than amusement as they scroll through social media posts. According to the Pew Research Center, more than 70 percent of US adults get at least some of their news from social media websites. Additionally, social media has become a hub for business interests. "Social media platforms are not only avenues for entertainment; they have become virtual marketplaces where consumers seek product information, reviews, and recommendations,"[1] says business technology consultant Harshal Karanpuriya. Not surprisingly, US businesses have created hundreds of thousands of new jobs to help capture their share of the burgeoning markets.

Seeking Engagement

By far the greatest source of social media–related employment is in the field of advertising. According to Statista Market Insights, a global data and business intelligence firm, companies spent $207 billion in the social media advertising market in 2023, with $72.3 billion being spent in the United States alone. Social media companies are benefiting directly from this ad spending, but so are digital marketing and communications companies. These firms create, place, and track the effectiveness of social media ads. Some businesses are also spending significant amounts of their marketing budgets to employ in-house digital marketing professionals to oversee and analyze their own social media advertising. The CMO Council, a global network of marketing executives, projects that social media marketing hiring will increase by 3.9 percent per year over the next several years as social media users spend increasing amounts of time browsing their favorite platforms, watching videos, posting pictures, and messaging friends.

Advertising is not the only method that companies are trying to increase engagement with social media users. Companies also post messages on microblogs, such as X (formerly Twitter) and Tumblr, with links back to content on their own websites. These links bolster business rankings on search engines, and the content builds customer satisfaction and loyalty.

To maximize the effectiveness of their campaigns, companies use various forms of data analytics to find out what their target audience is thinking, feeling, and saying about their brand in social media. Since the number of social media posts, comments, pictures, and even emojis is too large for any person or group of people to comprehend on their own, companies must use machines to collect, sort, and analyze the data. Hundreds of software companies have sprung up to produce digital tools that make sense of the social media data, including programs for social listening and sentiment analysis.

Companies are also hiring their own data scientists to create algorithms that analyze the vast amounts of social media data. Often, these data scientists use techniques known as machine learning and natural language processing to develop programs that can "understand" what is being said in social media and respond to it. These programs are often referred to as artificial intelligence, or AI. They can be used to tailor social media content to the interests of individual users. They can even engage with users directly through text messaging via chatbots.

A Bright Future

AI may someday perform some of the tasks being done by social media professionals today, but until then the social media industry will continue to be one of the fastest-growing sectors in the economy. Digital marketing may well see increased growth, but so will other jobs related to applications development, data analysis, and content creation. The Bureau of Labor Statistics does not track the growth of social media jobs separately, but it forecasts that overall employment in computer and information technology occupations will grow by 15 percent through 2031, much faster than the average for all occupations. This growth will result in about 682,800 new jobs over the decade. Because many of these jobs require computing and data science skills that relatively few people possess, those with the skills to make the most of social media activity will earn considerably more than the national average. As long as people continue to turn to social media for fun, relaxation, and information, the future of social media–related careers is bright.

Content Creator

What Does a Content Creator Do?

Social media content creators do the same things that social media users do: they post words, pictures, and videos to social media accounts. The difference is that social media creators do this for business purposes rather than for their own enjoyment, and they are paid for doing it.

In business these content creators often hold a position called a social media specialist. Some content creators work for digital media marketing firms that create social media campaigns for various business clients. In some cases content creators are self-employed "solopreneurs," contracting directly with their clients.

Not all clients are businesses. Some are nonprofit organizations, including government offices, schools, and churches. Others are individuals who need promotion—artists, musicians, authors, public speakers, and even politicians. Social media content creators are like social media influencers, but instead of building a following for themselves, they help build it for the company for which they work or the clients who pay them.

A Few Facts

Number of Jobs
About 9,100 in 2023

Pay
Median annual salary of $55,725

Educational Requirements
Bachelor's degree or equivalent

Personal Qualities
Excellent writing skills, highly organized, good time management

Work Settings
Indoors

Future Job Outlook
Growth rate of 10 percent through 2028

Typically, content creators are not marketing strategists. Branding and marketing strategies are determined by higher-ups and then handed down to marketing groups to execute. These groups include public relations, advertising, and sales support. Social media marketing is part of this mix. Social media content creators are responsible for carrying corporate messages into social media. All corporate communications, including social media posts, must follow the company's brand guidelines, which usually are documented in written form. The job of the social media content creator is to work within this corporate messaging framework to create engaging social media posts.

Often, social media messaging requires the content creator to insert hyperlinks to pages of their employer's or client's website. These links do more than guide readers to more information. They are also read by search engine robots, or bots, that examine websites and report the contents to the search engines. The search engines collect this link data and use it in their calculations for ranking websites. The more "in-links" a website has, the higher it will rank. When a social media post containing a link is shared many times, or goes viral, the number of links is greatly multiplied, improving the website's ranking. However, the links must be legitimate. They must be embedded in worthwhile content and be relevant to the post. Otherwise, search engines will penalize the website's ranking for illegitimate in-linking, often known as link farming. Savvy use of in-links is an important part of a content creator's job and a company's search engine optimization (SEO) strategy. "It's important to write for bots and for people," says Mandy Ison, group manager of holistic search for TurboTax. "The bot part is what writers and content producers don't usually know about or understand."[2]

Most social media content creators are writers. They develop written posts for Facebook, X, LinkedIn, Reddit, Quora, and others. However, they may also post pictures on Instagram, Tumblr, and Snapchat and videos on TikTok and YouTube. These pictures and videos often are created by other channels within a com-

Avoiding Burnout

"When I first started my TikTok content creator account, I was doing a 365-day series where I was sharing a social media tip every day for a year. By the time I got to around day 90, I was *so* burnt out and focused more on just getting a video out versus the quality of the content. I learned that while consistency is important on TikTok (and any other social platform), taking care of yourself is just as important. . . . When social media starts feeling like a chore, it shows through your content and ultimately performance will suffer."

—Courtney Park, social media manager in the tech field

Courtney Park, "A Day in the Life of Content Creator Courtney Park," Microsoft 365, April 5, 2023. https://create.microsoft.com.

pany or by the clients themselves. Many content creators are also photographers and videographers, and they create the posts by themselves. These individuals may even appear in visual media as models or spokespeople.

Unlike social media influencers, who have a free hand to post whatever they think will connect with their followers and promote the brands that sponsor them, content creators typically must submit their work for review by the corporate communications team. This may include not only marketing managers but also technical reviewers, who make sure the content is factually correct. In some cases the firm's legal team might need to be involved to make sure the public statements conform to laws and regulations.

The Workday

Social media content providers work in a variety of settings—at a corporation, as part of an agency, or as a self-employed freelancer—so it is not surprising that their workdays vary widely.

Working in Blocks of Time

"I decided to move to full-time content creation because that's where I had the most fun in my work. . . . I base my weekly schedule on the content projects I'm working on. It all depends on the form. If I'm writing, I work in two- to three-hour flow states. If it's a video project, I have to shoot during the day for optimal lighting. I can usually knock out filming in a few hours or so. . . . My administrative work depends on the project. . . . Long-term projects usually require check-ins through a weekly meeting or email."

—Jayde Powell, content creator and former social media manager

Quoted in Ronnie Gomez, "Content Creators: Who They Are, What They Do and How They Partner with Brands," Sprout Social, May 1, 2023. https://sproutsocial.com.

Even those who work directly for a corporation often work from home several days a week, and their daily schedules reflect this flexibility. Nevertheless, most social media content creators start the day by checking their email, replying to comments on their social media posts, and reviewing their calendar. They then plunge into content creation. "I usually don't have meetings in the morning, so this is when I'll do some deep work,"[3] says content creator Courtney Park.

Afternoons are often devoted to the administrative side of content creation: meetings, planning of future posts, and analysis of how the posts are performing. It is also important to respond to any emails or post comments that have come in during the day. Later afternoons can be used to tie up loose ends before heading home. "I typically lose steam around this time of day," says Joanna Hawley-McBride, a social media strategist and content creator, "so this is when I do low lift tasks like re-sharing old blog posts to social media, researching SEO opportunities, fixing broken parts of my website, and posting to Instagram stories."[4]

Education and Training

According to the online employment and recruitment service Zippia, 77 percent of full-time social media content creators have a bachelor's degree, while 10 percent have an associate's degree, and 7 percent have a master's degree. Only 3 percent have other degrees, and 3 percent have a high school diploma. Most employers are looking for candidates with a degree in English, communications, marketing, or business. However, a person who has experience in the company's industry might be considered as a content creator. For example, a person with retail experience in a particular industry might be able to use his or her product knowledge and customer service experience to craft suitable messages for a company in that industry. A person with an impressive portfolio of published work in journalism, advertising, or even on social media might be hired regardless of educational background.

Skills and Personality

Content creators must be skilled in writing above all, because nearly all corporate social media posts include text. Even videos featuring spokespeople or voice-over narration need to be written or at least outlined. Many content creators are also skilled in photography and videography. Some graphic design, video editing, and photo editing skills are also helpful for content creators who use visual media in their posts. Content creators must be able to work well in a team environment since they often receive message direction from upper management, are sent keyword and link information from SEO management, and may partner with graphic designers, photographers, and videographers to create content.

Working Conditions

Social media content creators who work for corporations or digital marketing companies usually work indoors in a casual environment and keep regular hours. Self-employed social media creators may work anywhere at any time, using their smartphones to create their posts. Many corporate social media creators work from home two or more days a week, often going into the office only for meetings.

Employers and Earnings

According to Zippia, 83 percent of content creators work for profit-making companies, 13 percent work for educational institutions, and 5 percent work for the government. Virtually all industries employ content creators. Media companies employ the most content creators—14 percent of all those working in the field. Start-up companies employ 12 percent, and education employs 11 percent. Internet companies and technology companies each employ 10 percent of social media content providers. Manufacturing (6 percent), government (4 percent), retail (4 percent), nonprofits (3 percent), and other industries each employ less than 10 percent of social media content creators.

Organizations of different sizes employ content creators at different rates. Organizations with more than a thousand employees employ 36 percent of content creators. Organizations with fifty to a thousand employees employ 52 percent of content creators. The remaining 12 percent are employed by organizations with fewer than fifty employees.

The online employment marketplace and recruitment platform ZipRecruiter reports that as of July 2023, the average annual salary for a social media content creator in the United States was $55,725 per year, well above the $36,200 median for all workers. The range in social media content creator salaries is wide, from about $25,000 to $95,000, but most positions pay $40,000 to $66,000 a year.

Zippia reports that salaries vary, depending on educational level. Content creators with a master's degree earn a median annual income of $69,864, while those with a bachelor's degree earn $63,878 annually. Those with an associate's degree earn $59,142 per year.

Future Outlook

According to the University of Texas at El Paso, content creation is a rapidly growing industry. The university forecasts a 10 percent increase in job growth through 2028. "The need for high-quality content is exploding," says Brian Benton, a self-employed content creator. "Companies are changing the way they think about content, which changes the type of work we're doing for them."[5]

Find Out More

American Marketing Association

www.ama.org

The American Marketing Association is a community for marketing professionals that offers certifications in digital marketing, content marketing, and marketing management. It also provides awards and scholarships at the college level and hosts online social media boot camps. Members receive discounts on webinars, conferences, and events.

Pexels

www.pexels.com

Pexels is a site used by some content creators. It has photos and videos that are free to use on blogs, websites, YouTube channels, and TikTok. As a courtesy, a user can give attribution to the photographer or videographer.

ProductionCrate

www.productioncrate.com

ProductionCrate is a website with free resources that creators or influencers can use to enhance their work. It offers visual effects and motion elements, sound effects, music, and graphics, including still images, video, 3-D and augmented reality, and plug-ins.

Social Media Influencer

What Does a Social Media Influencer Do?

Social media influencers are internet personalities who use their social media presence to promote products and brands. Most social media influencers build a following on their own and then team up with companies that want to present their brand or product to the influencer's followers. Many social media influencers gain prominence through the publication of videos on YouTube, TikTok, Instagram, and Twitch. Many influencers work in the health and fitness industry, promoting related products, including exercise gear, cosmetics, and clothing. But many popular and niche interests—from baking to video games—have influencers associated with them. And while some build their own brand, others work within the digital marketing team of a company or organization to push specific goods and services.

According to Statista Market Insights, companies will spend $4.92 billion in influencer advertising in the United States in 2023—more than double the amount companies spent just four years earlier. The reason for the growth in spend-

A Few Facts

Number of Jobs
About 1.5 million

Pay
Ranges from $1,000 to $100 million annually

Educational Requirements
No degree necessary

Personal Qualities
Self-confidence, ability to communicate well

Work Settings
Usually indoors but sometimes outdoors

Future Job Outlook
Growth rate of 44 percent through 2027

ing is simple: influencer advertising works. Advertisers know this because they can measure and track the effectiveness of social media influencers using tools provided by social media companies. "There is more demand from marketers because influencer advertising works so well in terms of return on investment (ROI) and organic engagement,"[6] says Statista.

The people who follow the influencers are much more engaged with their promotions than are people who see an ad on television that interrupts the programming. The followers watch the influencer's videos or read that individual's posts because they want to know what the influencer thinks. As a result, the followers are much more receptive to the influencer's product recommendations than they are to product pitches in other media.

Social media influencers provide access to the most sought-after audience: young adults who are forming their buying habits. This target audience is spending more of its time online, especially engaged with social media, than it ever has before. If advertisers are not reaching them through social media, they may not be reaching them at all.

The Workday

Social media influencers often work from home and set their own schedules. They might begin the day by checking their email and responding to comments on their most recent posts. Interaction with their followers is crucial because it builds connections with followers. "It's super important because it shows that you're a real person, not just some fantasy-unattainable-Instagram-thing,"[7] says influencer Caitlyn Warakomski.

Influencers usually spend the early morning planning the rest of the day and mapping out the content for the next few days, often with a social media management app like Planoly. If content is ready to be posted, the influencer will use the management app to post it at the time of day when it will receive the most views.

Influencers might also spend the morning producing their next video or photo shoot. This can include preparing wardrobe,

Making a Connection

"I began blogging during my lunch hour. . . . At the time I was blogging, it was very much looked down upon. It still is the kind of lowest of the low in the ecosystem of fashion. . . . The interesting thing about influencer culture is that it's very much a first-person perspective. You're talking about things from a subjective point of view. . . . I had more to gain than to lose by sharing. I also really believe in connection. Telling our stories is ultimately what makes us human and makes us feel like we connect and empathise."

—Camille Charrière, fashion influencer and columnist

Quoted in Muhammad Syed and Lily Heathcoat Amory, "Influencer Camille Charrière," *Varsity*, April 25 2023. www.varsity.co.uk.

---

lighting, camera positioning, and products they might be showcasing. After the shoot, they often go straight to editing to make sure the content is usable. They may have to do several takes to get the post right.

Influencers often have lunch with clients, potential advertisers, members of the press, and possible guests for future video segments. After lunch, influencers may visit showrooms to keep up-to-date on new products. Late afternoons are often devoted to more engagement with followers, responding to emails and comments. Dinner may be at home, or it may be with business contacts who are not available during the day. Sometimes the influencer will meet up with friends to socialize and to find out what topics are on their minds that might make good future posts.

Education and Training

Most social media influencers are self-employed. The companies that pay them to showcase their products do so on the strength of the influencers' social media following and their presentation skills, not because of any degrees or certifications they might have. While there are no official educational requirements that influencers must have, their followers expect them to be well spoken and be knowledgeable in their area. While this knowledge can be self-taught, having a postsecondary education can deepen an influencer's understanding of the subject, increasing that person's authority. For example, an influencer with a degree in fashion may be more credible and trustworthy when discussing fabric, workmanship, and design than someone who does not have a background in the industry.

Since social media influencers are really small business owners, a degree in business, finance, or marketing could help them build long-term success. Understanding the principles of business can help influencers negotiate with potential sponsors.

Skills and Personality

The most important skill for a social media influencer to have is the ability to communicate a viewpoint in a concise and entertaining way. Some influencers do this in writing only—through blogs, Facebook and X posts, and Instagram captions—but most do it through TikTok and YouTube videos. Regardless of the medium, the influencer needs good writing skills to create effective messages.

Influencers' technical skills depend on their chosen social media platform. TikTok and YouTube presenters need to have good video production skills. Instagram users must excel at photography and photo editing skills. Many bloggers enhance their written posts with photographs and videos, so they often develop skills in visual media as well.

The personality trait that nearly all influencers possess is self-confidence. It takes a belief in oneself to present one's thoughts, ideas, skills, and physical appearance to the public. It also requires confidence to contact potential sponsors and not give up when faced with rejection. Self-confidence is also important, because influencers must deal with criticism and even rudeness

Social media influencers are internet personalities who use their social media presence to promote products and brands. Many influencers build their own following and then team up with businesses that want to reach the influencer's followers.

from those who comment on their posts. Influencers need to be creative, stay organized, and have the self-discipline to meet deadlines and produce excellence even when they do not feel up to it. If they fail to post regularly, they will lose followers. "I know it's hard to post all the time and always capture content, but I think the more consistent you are, the better chances you have at succeeding," says social media influencer Arielle Charnas. "For me, and I'm sure for anyone, you go to an Instagram account, and if you don't see something different after two days, you're not going to go back to that account."[8]

Working Conditions

Social media influencers work in many different environments. Most work from home, setting up their digital cameras or video equipment in a room that relates to their specialty—the kitchen for diet and nutrition experts, the gym for health and exercise gurus, or a photo studio for fashion influencers. They often go on location to bring variety to their posts. Setting up photo and video equipment on location can be time consuming and expensive, however, so influencers must make sure their excursions make economic sense.

Social media influencers set their own hours, providing them with a great deal of flexibility. However, maintaining their own schedule can be a problem as well as a convenience. Social media influencers often feel that they never have downtime. They are always under pressure to do new posts and to comment on the places they go and things they do. "The most important thing is that this isn't a part-time job," says Huda Kattan, a beauty social media influencer. "When you leave the office on weekends, you are always going to be this person. You never get to leave that life."[9]

Employers and Earnings

Virtually any company can team up with social media influencers to build its brand. The leading industries investing in social media influencer advertising are cosmetics, fashion, food, nutrition,

An Around-the-Clock Job

"The hardest part is keeping up with it. You can't go on a week's vacation. It's every day, all day long. One of the biggest keys to success is building community and talking to people. But when you have over a million people following you on, like, six different platforms, responding to questions is a full-time job! Then you have the actual content creation: the photography element, the curation of imagery, shooting and editing video, writing a daily blog post. . . . It's a lot!"

—Kiersten Rich, travel and lifestyle blogger

Quoted in Ashlea Halpern, "Coolest Travel Jobs: What It's like to Be a Social Media Celebrity," *Afar*, October 6, 2017. www.afar.com.

movies, sports, and travel. Large companies often hire influencer marketing agencies to act as a go-between with the influencers. The agencies discover, contact, and select the most suitable influencers for the brand. They can also run the marketing campaigns, from developing creative strategies to reporting on the campaign's effectiveness. These agencies often work for the influencers as well, bringing them to the attention of the advertisers and making sure they are compensated fairly.

Among social media influencers who are employed by companies in the United States, the median annual salary is $57,561, according to an August 2023 survey by ZipRecruiter. The pay range is wide, from as low as $25,000 per year to as high as $93,599 per year.

According to Later, a company that produces social media management software, earnings vary even more widely among independent content creators. Creators with fewer than 100,000 followers can charge $100 to $1,000 per clip. Mid creators (100,000 to 500,000 followers) can charge between $1,500 and $5,000 per clip. Macro creators (over 500,000 followers) can charge $5,000 and up per clip.

Future Outlook

Later forecasts that ad spending on social media influencers will grow by 11 percent a year through 2027. This is much faster than the economy as a whole. While much of this spending will go to existing influencers, the number of social media influencers is expected to grow by 44 percent through 2027, much faster than the average for all occupations.

Find Out More

How to Start a YouTube Channel
https://youtu.be/e86l5j3GuPQ
This step-by-step tutorial from Jade Beason has a lot of helpful tips for beginners. Beason is a content creator, social media in-

fluencer, and social media consultant. Her YouTube channel has 130,000 subscribers and features more than 275 videos.

The Influencer Podcast
https://juliesolomon.net
The Influencer Podcast, hosted by Julie Solomon, provides inspiration, advice, and strategies on building an online following. Interviews with top influencers in a variety of spaces—including TikTok, YouTube, blogs, and social media—are available. The site offers more than five hundred episodes and more than three hundred guest interviews.

ProductionCrate
www.productioncrate.com
ProductionCrate is a website with free resources that creators or influencers can use to enhance their work. It offers visual effects and motion elements, sound effects, music, and graphics, including still images, video, 3-D and augmented reality, and plug-ins.

Artificial Intelligence Data Scientist

What Does an Artificial Intelligence Data Scientist Do?

With 4.9 billion active users spending an average of two hours and thirty-five minutes daily on various social media platforms, social media generates vast amounts of data. As a result, human beings cannot possibly analyze everything that is happening on social media that might be relevant for their businesses or institutions. They must use computers to make sense of all the data. Some computers use a process known as machine learning to make connections between various data and use the information to make predictions about future events. These programs are often referred to as artificial intelligence, or AI.

In the case of social media, AI can learn about an individual's preferences and behavior and then use this information to deliver personalized content that will most likely appeal to the user. For example, Instagram uses AI to serve up images that are similar to ones the user has "liked" in the past. This feature, known as Explore, creates greater

A Few Facts

Number of Jobs
About 159,630

Pay
Median annual salary of $117,065

Educational Requirements
Bachelor's degree or equivalent

Personal Qualities
Excellent math skills, analytical, able to work independently

Work Settings
Indoors

Future Job Outlook
Growth rate of 36 percent through 2031

engagement with the social media platform. Similarly, companies use AI to target advertising messages to various users based on their previous behavior. These ads are more likely to be effective than ads that are not targeted. The beauty of AI is that once the computer programmers have designed its operations and assigned its tasks, it can operate and make decisions without the help of human beings. AI is able to identify which posts and ads are most effective and use that information to improve its offerings across the platforms instantaneously.

A great deal of work goes into creating effective artificial intelligence. An AI program that works for Netflix advertising will not work for Nike advertising, for example. Companies and brands must develop or modify their AI programs to work for them. The people who do this work are known as artificial intelligence data scientists.

Data scientists turn unstructured data into structured data that can be used to meet business needs. Unstructured data can include posts, comments, likes, emojis, graphics interchange formats, maps, Global Positioning System readings, pictures, and videos. Because the data is not organized into specific categories, it is considered unstructured data. Structured data is information that has been organized and formatted into consistent categories. A Microsoft Excel spreadsheet's content is an example of structured data. Each record is represented by a horizontal line on the spreadsheet and divided into separate cells that capture different data. Data scientists use software tools to turn masses of unstructured data into organized data sets. They can then program a computer to use the structured data to make predictions. For example, AI can organize the English language into parts of speech and then use various texts to "teach" the computer what words normally follow other words, according to the rules of language. When a person is chatting in a text box, the AI program might predict what words normally will follow what the person has typed. This type of predictive analysis can be used by chatbots to answer questions a customer might have. As the chat proceeds, the machine is learning what works and what does not work in the dialogue. A data scientist can look at reports about how the program is working and find ways to make it work better.

The Workday

There is tremendous variety in what a data scientist does. What a data scientist does on a particular day depends on where the project stands. If it is at the beginning, the data scientist will need to formulate the questions that the AI program needs to answer. The data scientist will then collect data from different sources and organize it in a way that could answer the questions.

Once an AI model has been created, it must be tested to see whether it is viable. Even if it works, the data scientists must be able to estimate the costs of implementation to see whether the project makes sense from a business perspective. Data scientists must coordinate their work with others, including database administrators, who are responsible for the design, implementation, maintenance, and modification of databases. As a result, data scientists often start the day by checking in with their colleagues. "For a data scientist, a typical day depends on the phase of the project one is working on," says Sadaf Sayyad, a data scientist for Intuit. "But, on a high level, my day starts with checking emails and messages for any urgent tasks. Then, we have a stand-up meeting to discuss the progress of the project . . . followed by planning my day."[10]

Data scientists typically spend the rest of their time working on their projects. This can include gathering data, merging it, and analyzing it. This is done using a variety of database tools. The data scientist will also develop and test new algorithms to create functioning AI programs. Each new algorithm needs to be tested to see whether it yields the desired results. The data scientist will look for patterns and trends to troubleshoot and solve problems. "Data scientists are primarily problem solvers," says Eshna Verma, a senior manager at Simplilearn. "Working with this data also

Every Challenge Is Different

"The challenge and beauty of being a data scientist are that every problem you get is likely different. Therefore, the single approach most likely will not work for two problems. This makes our job very exciting as every project is a new learning opportunity. We build the first version model/solution as a proof of concept to ensure there is merit in pursuing a project. Then, suppose the target metrics look positive, and the cost of building and maintaining a model is worth the benefit. In that case, we go ahead to build out a production-level model."

—Sadaf Sayyad, data scientist at Intuit

Quoted in Amit Raja Naik, "A Day in the Life of a Data Scientist: Impacting People's Lives Through the Power of AI," AIM, April 1, 2022. https://analyticsindiamag.com.

means understanding the goal. Data scientists must also seek to determine the questions that need answers and then come up with different approaches to try and solve the problem."[11]

Education and Training

To be considered for an entry-level position in the artificial intelligence field, candidates need at least a bachelor of science degree in data analytics, data management, or computer science. This provides a foundation for turning unstructured data into usable information. It will also familiarize candidates with tools that allow them to perform in-depth data analysis. Typically, a data scientist will have at least a master of science degree and possibly a doctoral degree in data analytics. An advanced degree will familiarize the student with statistics and statistical procedures, data clustering, hypothesis testing, computer vision, and natural language processing. Students learn how to map out decision trees that use a series of questions to split data into usable categories. They learn to use advanced data mining and analytics

Coming Up with Creative Solutions

"My favorite part of the job is creating a plan of attack for a new problem: envisioning the steps necessary to take raw data and put it into a form that gives meaningful, actionable knowledge to the client. That's when I usually discover the most interesting new technologies, techniques, and models, and get to come up with the most creative ways to use those methods to process data given available resources. . . . The most challenging part of the job, of course, is finding the source of a bug that is causing all of your model outputs to be nonsensical."

—James M. Tobin, writer, researcher, and editor

James M. Tobin, "Typical Day of a Data Scientist," ComputerScience.org, August 1, 2023. www.computerscience.org.

tools, including Hadoop, Spark, PROC SQL, and more. Since most databases are stored on networked servers known as "the cloud," data scientists need to be skilled in using cloud platforms such as Google Cloud.

Certification is not a requirement for hiring in most settings, but it can help a candidate land a highly desirable job because it is proof that the data scientist is proficient in advanced AI techniques. For example, IBM offers certification in Python for data science. The Artificial Intelligence Board of America offers certification for an artificial intelligence engineer. The online tech company Coursera offers a certificate program that covers best practices for using TensorFlow, an open-source machine learning framework.

Skills and Personality

Artificial intelligence data scientists need to have strong analytical abilities, exceptional math skills, and the ability to think logically. They also need relevant technical skills, with proficiency in AI software and database tools. AI data scientists must be self-starters who are willing to take the initiative to solve problems. While AI data scientists must be comfortable working independently, they also must have good communication skills to document their work and explain their concepts and progress to nontechnical executives. They need good writing skills, especially if they are working with virtual agents or chatbots.

Working Conditions

Artificial intelligence data scientists work indoors at a desk with a computer. Data scientists in large corporations typically work in a highly structured environment with dress codes and regular hours. Those who work for digital marketing firms often work in a more casual environment with more flexible hours. Some may work at home a few days a week, using virtual private networks to run tests on remote databases in the cloud.

Employers and Earnings

Companies in a wide range of industries use AI to deliver personalized social media content to their target audiences. The social media platforms themselves employ AI data scientists to increase user engagement and satisfaction with AI apps that serve up tailored suggestions for new individuals and groups for users to follow.

AI data scientists are highly sought after, and their salaries reflect their market clout. According to an August 2023 survey by PayScale, a compensation software and data company, the average salary for a data scientist with artificial intelligence skills is $117,065 a year. The salary ranges from $79,000 to $151,000 a year. AI data scientists can also earn annual bonuses from $2,000 to $16,000. Some companies also have profit sharing plans that provide further compensation if the company hits its profit targets. PayScale estimates the profit sharing to range from $750 to $9,000 per year.

Future Outlook

According to the Bureau of Labor Statistics (BLS), employment of data scientists is projected to grow by 36 percent through 2031. This growth rate is greater than the average for all other occupations. The BLS projects that there will be 13,500 openings for data scientists each year until 2031. "The ability to take data—to be able to understand it, to process it, to extract value from it, to visualize it, to communicate it—that's going to be a hugely important skill in the next decades,"[12] says Hal Varian, a University of California, Berkeley, professor of information sciences, business, and economics.

Find Out More

Data Science Central

www.datasciencecentral.com

Described as a community for big data practitioners, this site lists newsletters, podcasts, videos, and webinars relevant to data fields. In addition to sections on social media and AI, other foci include AI ethics, trends, data privacy, and strategy.

Kaggle

www.kaggle.com

Kaggle is a data science community recently acquired by Google. The site has a blog, and the community offers mentorship, competitions, and forums, as well as models and datasets for developers. The site offers courses, which are free, and students can earn certificates.

Women in Data Science (WiDS)

www.widsconference.org

WiDS is an international community offering visitors access to conferences, lectures, seminars, datathons, podcasts, and blogs. The Next Gen program is an initiative of WiDS that supports high school students who are interested in data science careers.

Social Media Manager

What Does a Social Media Manager Do?

Promoting brands and products across social media platforms requires strategic thinking, planning, and coordination. The person responsible for a company's effective use of social media is a social media manager. The position combines analytical capabilities with team leadership skills. The social media manager analyzes data about social media engagement and uses it to direct the posting of social media content to achieve maximum impact and results. The social media manager creates reports to monitor progress and communicate progress to upper management.

The Workday

With so many responsibilities, social media managers tend to break their days up into blocks of time to concentrate on each specific task without getting distracted. Many social media managers start the day by checking messages and emails from their coworkers so they can respond to any unscheduled items that have come up and plan for any needed meetings. They then check the day's content calendar to see what is scheduled to be published across the various platforms that day.

A Few Facts

Number of Jobs
About 27,000

Pay
Median annual salary of $56,500

Educational Requirements
Bachelor's degree or equivalent

Personal Qualities
Excellent people skills, analytical, able to think and communicate verbally and visually

Work Settings
Indoors

Future Job Outlook
Growth rate of 10 percent through 2031

With the day's plan in mind, a social media manager will check to see whether the content has been created and is ready to go. This can include editing posts that are scheduled for publication. Many social media managers engage with the community directly, setting aside time to check their social media inboxes and respond to followers. They not only reply to messages, they also repost interesting information. "The most important and productive times for me throughout the day are when I can do focus work, which includes creating content, working on upcoming posts in the content calendar, scheduling posts . . . , and engaging with the community,"[13] says Mitra Mehvar, a social media manager for Buffer, a social media management platform.

Some social media managers are responsible for posting to the company's blog. Often, they will survey the day's events to see whether they should write a post or make a video responding to current events or go ahead with a planned blog post.

Afternoons are often set aside for meetings to gather input from team members and brainstorm new ideas. Social media managers will also perform data analysis on their own campaigns. They might even find time to research trending hashtags to see what is hot in their field and monitor their competitors' activities.

Most social media managers will do another check of email and incoming messages to respond to emerging issues. As the day winds down, the social media manager may scroll through social media looking for inspiration. "I intentionally build researching, learning, creating, and engaging time into my day," says Mehvar. "I know that it might look like I'm trying to get out of working when I say I'm 'scrolling through TikTok for research'—but I really am doing it for research!"[14] Before leaving for the day, social media managers will check that all scheduled posts were completed and take a quick look at what is scheduled for the next day.

Education and Training

Companies searching for a qualified social media manager typically look for candidates who hold a bachelor's degree in a field

Data Analysis

"Much of social media management is reviewing KPIs [key performance indicators] to evaluate just how social media posts are performing. The goal of social media marketing for most companies is to increase the organic reach of a company's posts, so it's important to have a good idea of how each post is expanding beyond a company's account. Reviewing results from testing, seeing what posts are encouraging interactions from your current customers, and which ones are attracting new ones are all part of a social media manager's daily analysis of active posts, so they can make informed decisions about what will post next on a company's account."

—Kyle Risley, founder of Lift Vault

Quoted in Stukent, "A Day in the Life of a Social Media Manager," August 30, 2022. www.stukent.com.

---

that emphasizes the fundamentals of communications and business, including marketing, public relations, and journalism. Some employers may expect candidates to have earned certifications from the major players in the digital technology environment, including Meta and Google. These certifications might include the Meta Social Media Marketing Professional Certificate or the Google Data Analytics Professional Certificate. Certifications from companies focused on social media strategy and analytics, including HubSpot and Hootsuite, can also prove a candidate's working knowledge of social media management.

Most employers expect social media managers to have some kind of track record in social media success. This can include work experience in an entry-level position such as social media associate or digital content producer. It could also mean a portfolio of work built by volunteering for an organization that needs to build a presence online. Since many tools for social media analysis are

Social media managers promote brands and products across social media platforms, a job that requires strategic thinking, planning, and coordination. They take part in company meetings and set aside time to directly engage with followers.

available online at no charge, anyone can gain experience—and show verifiable results—by building and documenting a social media presence for an organization, individual, or event.

Skills and Personality

An effective social media manager needs a blend of hard skills—technical and mathematical skills—and soft skills, including communication and leadership skills. On the technical side, a social media manager needs to know not only how to use social media platforms but also how to schedule the release of new content across the various platforms. For example, they might need to know how to combine an influencer's TikTok video with their own company's video, a process known as *stitching*, or post their company's video side by side with another video in TikTok, a process known as *dueting*. A social media manager also must be an expert at using analytics tools—such as Hootsuite, Sprout Social, and Zoho Social—to measure engagement with the employer's social media campaign. A social media manager also needs to track and understand the impact of current events and cultural trends on the social media environment. "Social media managers often search news websites and social media to find out about breaking news and trending topics related to the company's industry," says Dustin Ray of Incfile, a national document filing service. "For example, a social media manager working for a beauty brand could search TikTok or YouTube for the latest juice from renowned beauty influencers. They might decide to stitch or duet the video on TikTok or add clips on their YouTube video to add context and commentary."[15]

Since social media is often the place where a person will first hear about a company or its products and services, the social media manager must have excellent communication and writing skills. The social media manager must be able to direct the content creators to develop messages that reflect the company's values and brand. The social media manager will also edit the content so it makes the best possible impression on the audience. "Social media managers have to look through every small edit and mistake to see if it is fixed in the right way," says Anthony King, a social media manager for Transport Executive. The ability to evaluate and edit applies not only to the verbal messages but also to the visual ones; therefore, a knowledge of graphic design is essential. Finally, the social media manager must have the leadership skills to inspire the social media team to create a successful social media presence. "I am a massive people person, so I love interacting with and supporting various contacts across the group," says Emily-Sian Barker, a social media manager at RSK Group. "Usually these connections work within social media, so it's great to empower and bounce off like-minded, passionate individuals."[16]

Working Conditions

Social media managers work indoors. Before the COVID-19 pandemic, most social media managers worked in an office setting. During the pandemic most worked from home. Now both options are available, but many social media managers combine the two, working from home most of the week but coming into the office for meetings once or twice a week. Occasionally, social media managers will travel to attend social media marketing conferences to gain deeper insight into the market and learn business-building techniques.

Employers and Earnings

Organizations that market to consumers—as opposed to other businesses—are the biggest users of social media. According to the social media analytics firm Rival IQ, media companies were the most frequent posters of content on Facebook, Twitter, and TikTok in 2022. Sports teams were the most active organizations on Instagram and the second-most active on Facebook and Twitter. On TikTok health and beauty, fashion, and retail companies were second, third, and fourth, respectively, behind media companies. Sports teams were the fifth-most active posters on TikTok but had a higher rate of engagement (including likes, comments, and favorites) than the more active posters on the platform. However, the highest engagement rate by far on TikTok was earned by higher education institutions. They garnered a 16 percent engagement rate per video, compared to a 9 percent engagement rate for sports teams and an average of 5.7 percent engagement rate across all industries. Higher education also had the highest engagement rate on Instagram, with sports teams leading the way on Twitter and Facebook.

According to PayScale, the median salary of a social media manager is $56,500 a year, ranging from a low of $38,000 to a high of $85,000 a year. Some companies provide bonuses of up to $9,000 for outstanding performance. Other firms offer profit sharing of up to $11,000. Location has a big impact on the salaries of social media managers. Social media managers in Austin, Texas, earn 37 percent more than the national average, according to PayScale. Social media managers earn 24 percent more than the national average in San Francisco, 21 percent more in Seattle, and

> ### Interacting with the Social Media Audience
>
> "The days of advertising as a one-way conversation are long gone. The most successful brands today are those who engage in two-way dialogue with their customers. They assist you in establishing, growing, and managing social media communities—from Twitter and Facebook to LinkedIn, Pinterest, and Instagram—as well as engaging followers with relevant material. In other words, they assist in the development of relationships and the promotion of brand loyalty."
>
> —Anthony King, social media manager
>
> Quoted in "What Does a Marketing Agency Do?" Terkel, May 9, 2023. https://blog.terkel.io.

16 percent more in Washington, DC. Social media specialists in Minneapolis earn about 16 percent less than the national average.

Future Outlook

Social media managers are in demand as companies compete for the attention of users who engage with these platforms daily. The job forecast is positive, with a projected growth rate of 10 percent through 2031. That growth is faster than the average for all occupations.

Find Out More

American Marketing Association
www.ama.org
The American Marketing Association is a community for marketing professionals that offers certifications in digital marketing, content marketing, and marketing management. It also provides awards and scholarships at the college level and hosts online social media boot camps. Members receive discounts on webinars, conferences, and events.

Social Media Club

http://socialmediaclub.org

With chapters in several large cities, the Social Media Club's mission is to promote media literacy and standard technologies, encourage ethical behavior, and share best practices among social media professionals. The organization's website contains links to several club blogs and social media events, as well as general educational materials.

Social Media Professional Association

www.certificationinsocialmedia.com

The Social Media Professional Association is an organization that provides training, education, and certification in social media marketing. Its website contains links to articles and research about social media in a marketing context.

Social Media Today

www.socialmediatoday.com

Social Media Today is an independent online community for professionals in public relations, marketing, advertising, and other disciplines that rely on social media. The website hosts lively debates about the tools, platforms, companies, and personalities that are revolutionizing the way information is consumed. Articles are contributed by professionals who work with social media.

Association of National Advertisers (ANA)

https://www.ana.net

The ANA is the US advertising industry's oldest and largest trade association. It supports professionals working in all types of advertising, including social media marketing. Its website contains information about best practices, regulations, and opportunities within digital media. Various online publications, including its *Industry Insights* blog, are available to nonmembers at no cost.

Mobile App Developer

What Does a Mobile App Developer Do?

An amazing 99 percent of the world's 4.48 billion social media users access websites or apps through a mobile device. Not surprisingly, the applications, or apps, developed for social media are designed to run best on mobile devices. "In today's interconnected world, where smartphones have become an essential part of our daily lives, the demand for mobile applications is skyrocketing," says business technology consultant Harshal Karanpuriya. "Whether it's for business, entertainment, or utility purposes, mobile apps have revolutionized the way we interact with technology."[17]

The skills for mobile app development are different from those for developing software that runs mainly on other computers. The people who create, test, and develop apps for smartphones and tablets are known as mobile app developers. They work in popular operating system environments like iOS and Android. They write, test, and debug code for mobile applications. "As an app developer, you get to be at the heart of developing a mobile solution," says Ahmed Joni, a freelance search engine optimization specialist and app developer. "You get to

A Few Facts

Number of Jobs
About 1.6 million

Pay
Median annual salary of $78,255

Educational Requirements
Bachelor's degree or equivalent

Personal Qualities
Excellent coding skills, analytical, able to solve problems creatively

Work Settings
Indoors

Future Job Outlook
Growth rate of 25 percent through 2031

experience all parts of developing an app, right from the initial idea through to final deployment into the app store."[18]

Mobile app developers can perform a variety of duties, depending on the needs of their employer. In some cases they will develop a brand-new app to help mobile users perform a task, play a game, or gather information in a new way. Sometimes they will modify an existing desktop app to make it compatible with mobile devices, including phones, tablets, and wearables. However, mobile apps are not just desktop apps formatted for small screens. The mobile web developer must make sure the app makes sense to a mobile device user.

The world of social media is constantly changing, and mobile app developers are often required to update existing apps to meet new requirements. For example, government officials sometimes pass laws that set new parameters for the use of social media data. Existing social media apps will have to be updated within a specific time frame to comply with the new laws. Apps also must be optimized to meet new security challenges. This can involve adapting to emerging threats, but also it can mean making sure that data is secure as mobile apps are linked to the company's existing network.

The Workday

Some mobile app developers work for themselves and earn money from sales of their apps to consumers. In such cases they spend most of their day coding features for a new app or updating existing apps. They also monitor statistics generated by the apps to make sure the apps are working as intended.

Most mobile app developers, though, work for companies and are part of app development teams. As a result, mobile app developers often kick off their day by meeting with the team members in person or via video calls. "Every day we have a quick catch up as a team to talk about anything that might be on our mind," explains Heather Kay, a mobile app developer with Manchester Digital. "These . . . are a great way of keeping connected

Advantages of a Humanities Education

"My liberal arts education forced me to see the world from other people's perspectives, which is a goal of the study of the humanities. Empathy, or being able to put oneself in other people's shoes, is an important trait for many reasons. Empathy allows engineers to better understand their users' pain points so they can build software products that more precisely address that pain. On a more philosophical level, empathy invites engineers to question the ethical implications of what they build—for example, do they want to use their programming skills to create a product that intentionally spreads false news."

—Hou Chia, software engineer

Hou Chia, "Getting into Programming as a Humanities Graduate," LinkedIn, March 4 2021. www.linkedin.com.

even when we're working from home and keeping open lines of communication if we have any issues."[19]

The rest of the day is spent writing code and testing it to see whether it is performing properly. If it is, the code is uploaded into the repository of all the code generated by the team for the specific project. App developers are often assigned "tickets" to perform specific tasks, including fixing software glitches, or bugs; researching new technologies that might be relevant to the company's apps; and writing documentation for the apps.

Education and Training

Most companies expect a mobile app developer to have an undergraduate degree in computer science, software engineering, or another information technology (IT) field. Many students planning to develop mobile apps study software engineering, gaining knowledge of data management and programming. However, Dina Destreza, a product development expert in user interface design, believes that good mobile app developers need a broader background than just programming. "An engineer with a background in humanities would build a unique product, which can easily bring in the 'Wow!' factor. Whereas an engineer with a background in engineering ends up developing a copy of another product, which lacks originality,"[20] writes Destreza.

Many social media apps access data stored online in groups of networked computers known as the cloud. Some apps have a user interface on the mobile device but perform some or all of their operations in the cloud. Companies with cloud-based apps will be interested in hiring mobile app developers with a degree in cloud computing.

Many companies see certification in mobile app development as proof of a candidate's ability to start developing apps from the first day on the job. Meta offers both a Meta Android Developer Professional Certificate and a Meta iOS Developer Professional Certificate. Meta has teamed up with Coursera to offer a Meta React Native Specialization Certificate that helps developers create apps that utilize native device features, including the device's camera, microphone, Global Positioning System, and more. Coursera, in collaboration with Vanderbilt University, offers a certificate in Android App Development Specialization, which focuses on creating mobile apps made up of core Android components. Apple offers a curriculum teaching Swift, a programming language created by Apple for building apps for iOS. Swift certification is available through an exam administered by Certiport. Since 90 percent of mobile apps are written for iOS or Android operating systems, employers prefer candidates with application development for these environments.

Skills and Personality

Mobile app developers need to be creative thinkers when it comes to planning what an app should do and methodical in the creation of software code. They often work in teams, so they need to be able to work well with other app developers, database

Mobile app developers create brand-new apps and update existing ones. They also modify desktop apps to make them more user-friendly and compatible with mobile devices.

professionals and other IT staff, executives, and everyone else connected with a project.

For technical skills, they need to be proficient in web development basics, including JavaScript, HTML, and CSS. Those basics will allow an app developer to create a good user interface and then make the interface, or front end, communicate with databases in networked computers, or the back end. Once familiar with the coding basics, the mobile app developer will need to become fluent in the programming languages for mobile devices. Most developers for Apple devices use Swift. Most Android developers have used Java, the official development language for Android, but Kotlin has become popular due to its flexibility and ease of use. Although some mobile app developers work in both Apple and Android environments, it is much more common to specialize in one or the other.

After creating a mobile app, developers need to know how to test it to identify and fix bugs or inconsistencies. They also must

Developing Social Media Apps for Wearables

"Wearable technology has become increasingly popular in recent years, and it's no surprise that it has found its way into the realm of social media. . . . With wearable technology, we can receive notifications, check messages, and even interact with social media platforms without having to pull out our smartphones. This seamless integration allows us to stay connected while on the go, providing a new level of convenience and accessibility. For example, imagine being able to quickly glance at your smartwatch to see the latest social media updates or track your engagement metrics without interrupting your daily activities."

—Royale Kassandra, tech writer

Royale Kassandra, "Connecting the Dots: How Hardware Innovations Are Revolutionizing Social Media," All You Can Leet, June 19, 2023. https://allyoucanleet.com.

ensure that the methods they are using to work with a company's database files are streamlined and secure.

Working Conditions

Mobile app developers work indoors, often in a casual environment. "I like our working environment because it is friendly and open," says mobile app developer Vilma Un Jan. "We share a space with other companies, so there are common areas where we can decompress with things like a pool table, a game room, and comfy chairs to relax."[21]

Most mobile app developers are full-time employees who often work long hours to meet deadlines. Because application coding and testing normally can be performed on laptop computers, mobile app developers can work virtually anywhere. As a result, many work from home or other locations at least a few days a month.

Employers and Earnings

Some mobile app developers contract independently with companies to develop or update apps according to the company's needs. Others work within companies that provide technical assistance to larger businesses. In the field of social media, many mobile app developers are part of the social media platform's staff. The major industries hiring mobile app developers include social media companies, technology research firms, health care organizations, nonprofit organizations, and mobile phone research companies.

According to PayScale, the average mobile app developer earns $78,255 a year. The pay range is from about $54,000 on the low end to about $128,000 at the high end. Salaries vary depending on several factors, including the employer's size and location and the developer's education, certifications, and years of experience. Mobile app developers earn 25.2 percent more than the national average in San Francisco, 12 percent more than the national average in New York, and 5 percent more in Austin, Texas. At the low end, mobile app developers in Atlanta earn 19 percent less than the national average, and those in Philadelphia earn 13.3 percent less than the national average.

Future Outlook

The Bureau of Labor Statistics (BLS) estimates that employment opportunities for software developers are expected to increase by 25 percent through 2031, creating 411,400 new positions. This forecasted growth rate is much faster than the average across all occupations. The BLS says this growth results from the increasing need for new apps to accommodate mobile device users. "Having a mobile app allowed many companies to stay in business and operate during the pandemic," observes Ronald Renaud, a self-employed marketing research analyst. "Therefore, as long as there are smartphones, mobile application development will be in demand."[22]

Find Out More

App Developers Alliance

http://appdevelopersalliance.org

The App Developers Alliance supports developers through education, advocacy, and leadership. It also works to raise the profile of developers among policy makers, the business community, and the media. The alliance's website includes white papers, research, infographics, and best practice guides.

App Quality Alliance (AQuA)

www.appqualityalliance.org

AQuA is a global association focused on helping the industry continually improve and promote mobile app quality across all platforms. AQuA acts as a referral and endorsement body, accrediting the quality of developers and their apps. The organization offers developers tools to test their apps for common errors, accessibility, and network performance.

Association of Software Professionals (ASP)

https://asp-software.org

The ASP was a professional trade association of software developers who created desktop and laptop programs, service applications, cloud computing software, and mobile apps. The association was dissolved in 2020, but its website is maintained and still makes available its library of twenty-five years of newsletter articles and more than five years of member-to-member discussions.

Social Media Intelligence Analyst

What Does a Social Media Intelligence Analyst Do?

While social media focuses on communicating with users, some social media professions examine the business side of the industry by poring over the constant traffic to note trends. Companies must be aware of not only what their own efforts are achieving but also what their competitors are doing. They also need to know what potential risks or threats exist for their business. The person who monitors online chatter for trends and threats is known as an intelligence analyst. "We cover the behind the scenes of what you see in your feed," says Kate O'Hagan, senior specialist of social media intelligence at United Airlines. "We monitor online chatter for any trends and threats to the airline . . . brand."[23]

Intelligence analysts are not always playing defense, however. They also are on the lookout for opportunities that might arise from the actions of their competitors. They find ways to insert the brand into the online activities of others, including social media influencers and partner organizations, to promote the

A Few Facts

Number of Jobs
About 100,000

Pay
Median annual salary of $71,371

Educational Requirements
Bachelor's degree or equivalent

Personal Qualities
Excellent people skills, analytical, able to think and communicate visually

Work Settings
Indoors

Future Job Outlook
Growth rate of 19 percent through 2031*

*For market research analysts, including social media intelligence analysts

brand. For example, they might identify a charitable organization that their company could sponsor to help build goodwill.

Social media intelligence analysts are responsible for monitoring activity on all social media platforms, not just social networking sites like Facebook and LinkedIn. Important competitive information can be found on media-sharing sites like Instagram and Pinterest; video sharing sites like TikTok and YouTube; microblogging platforms like X and Tumblr; and social gaming platforms like Twitch, Xbox Live, Game Center, Discord, and Steam. A social media intelligence analyst will also follow related blogs to learn what insiders are saying. They often engage in a type of data analysis known as sentiment analysis, to quantify how social media users, customers, and competitor customers are feeling about a wide range of issues. "When you're social listening, you're not just providing a solution to a problem. You're showing that your brand views its customers as human beings, not just an opportunity for a sale," says We Make Heart, a digital marketing firm. "Social listening means honing a keen ear and tone for developing a human brand voice."[24]

Although social media intelligence analysts may dip into various social media accounts to personally take the temperature of the user environment, they cannot rely on their own data gathering to identify trends and sentiments. They need to use a specially designed social listening platform such as Sprinklr, Sprout Social, or Mention, or they can use a social media management platform that has its own social listening tools, such as Brandwatch, Hootsuite, Falcon.io, Radian6, Sysomos, or NetBase Quid. "Social listening allows for opportunities to identify what consumers care about, any pain points they may have, and provides context into how to best speak to them through social media,"[25] says Jessica Hammerstein, a social media intelligence analyst with Ignite Social Media, a digital marketing firm.

Keeping tabs on social media trends is only part of the job for social media intelligence analysts. They use the power of social listening to inform and influence their company's marketing and

Constant Change

"There is no 'normal day' in social media intelligence. It all depends on what's going on with the airline. We also run sentiment analysis reports on certain things for potential upcoming projects. For example, if we wanted to partner with a celebrity, we look into their history and what the internet thinks of the person to see if it's a good match for our brand."

—Kate O'Hagan, senior analyst of social media intelligence at United Airlines

Quoted in Ronnie Gomez, "Social Media Careers: The Skills You Need, Where to Look and Jobs to Consider," Sprout Social, July 7, 2022. https://sproutsocial.com.

business decisions. They discover what is important to the company's social communities and then connect the dots between the consumer and the brand. They communicate their observations and insights to their colleagues in the business, presenting quantified reports and actionable plans. For example, a social media intelligence analyst working for a retailer can help managers make difficult decisions about their inventory by using social media intelligence to decide what to discount and what might be better to keep at full price.

The Workday

The first thing social media intelligence analysts need to do is receive and validate new intelligence information from a variety of data gathering tools. Their analysis cannot begin until they are fully updated on emerging trends and potential concerns. Hammerstein says:

> On a day-to-day basis, a significant part of my job is to collect, aggregate, and analyze data from many different sources in order to confidently report on where a brand

stands in the social space. This involves getting real comfortable with analytics tools (Facebook Insights, Twitter Analytics, YouTube Analytics, Google Analytics, etc.) and paid media reporting tools (Facebook Ads Manager/Power Editor, Twitter Ads, etc.), as well as third-party social analytics tools in order to pull all relevant social data relating to channel and content performance.[26]

Once the data has been collected and updated, a social media intelligence analyst will search for patterns, trends, and abnormalities that may need further review. The analyst is always on the lookout for interesting words and phrases that people are using when discussing a brand on social networks, blogs, forums, and news sites. This information can be passed along to other members of the social media team to help promote the brand. The analyst may prepare a written assessment of the day's developments, including graphs, maps, or charts.

The analyst may report information in daily or weekly meetings, often scheduled for the afternoon so the day's new information has been collected and analyzed. If the analyst identifies increased social media engagement around a particular story or sentiment, the information will be shared with content producers so they can work it into their communications as quickly as possible. If the analyst detects negative sentiment or chatter about a product or aspect of the brand, this information also must be shared quickly to kick-start a response.

Education and Training

To become a social media intelligence analyst, you typically need a bachelor's degree in a field such as marketing, communications, journalism, or business administration. Some employers may require a master's degree in one of the communications or business fields. Qualified candidates need to have excellent math skills and a basic understanding of database analytics.

Social media intelligence analysts monitor online chatter for trends and threats. They also pore over online traffic to note trends involving competitors.

The McAfee Institute offers the Certified Social Media Intelligence Expert, a nationally accredited certification course to help candidates gain theoretical and hands-on experience in social media intelligence gathering. The Yale School of Management also offers a certified online course in digital marketing that includes modules devoted to social media listening, promotion, and engagement.

Skills and Personality

Social media intelligence combines several disciplines—communications, marketing, technology, and analytics. A social media intelligence analyst should have experience with tools and techniques for collecting, collating, and analyzing information about existing or potential markets and market needs. "A career in social media intelligence might be right for you if you live and breathe data," says Ronnie Gomez, a content strategist at Sprout

Turning Data into a Story

"Because staring at an Excel spreadsheet full of numbers can be confusing and anxiety-inducing for many right-brained individuals, reporting is also an essential role of an analyst. We need to be able to identify key insights and information, visualize the data, and provide context in a way that is digestible and easy to understand. We also need to be able to analyze prior data in order to provide realistic goals and benchmarks on a client-by-client basis, so the internal team and client have a clear understanding of what makes a KPI's performance . . . 'good.'"

—Jessica Hammerstein, analyst at Ignite Social Media

Jessica Hammerstein, "A Day in the Life of a Social Media Analyst," Ignite Social Media, March 31, 2023. www.ignitesocialmedia.com.

Social. "You enjoy poring over large data sets to identify trends and opportunities."[27]

A social media intelligence analyst is often the first person to detect threats to a company's reputation and brand. As such, they must know how to remain calm under pressure so they can respond effectively to mitigate a crisis before it happens. This includes using social listening software and social media management tools to accurately assess the scope and seriousness of a problem before mapping out a strategy to counteract it.

Social media intelligence analysts must be able to effectively communicate their findings to various stakeholders and audiences. They need good writing skills to summarize their activities in daily, weekly, monthly, and quarterly social listening reports. These reports often include recommendations for actions that can be taken to address concerns and exploit opportunities. Analysts also need to be able to communicate data in reports using spreadsheets created by programs like Microsoft Excel.

While the position is mostly technical, social media intelligence analysts are part of a large team. They need to be a team player and enjoy collaborating with the social media team, creative team, marketing operations, and other brand-marketing teams. They also need good time-management and project-management skills to plan, organize, and execute social listening campaigns to meet goals and objectives.

Working Conditions

The working conditions for a social media intelligence analyst depend on the company and industry. Social media intelligence analysts typically work regular hours in office settings so they can coordinate with their coworkers in marketing, advertising, and data analytics departments. As in many hi-tech settings, the dress code tends to be casual, and employees sometimes work from home on some weekdays.

Employers and Earnings

Many for-profit and nonprofit industries use social media intelligence. While every company's brand is important to it, companies in the financial sector—including banking, financial services, and insurance—have the most to lose if their reputation is damaged by rumors or negative reports in social media. Other industries that are heavy users of social media intelligence include retail, e-commerce, information technology, telecommunications, and media.

According to Glassdoor, the salary range for a social media intelligence analyst is from $44,000 to $116,000 per year in the United States. Glassdoor reports that the median estimated total pay for a social media intelligence analyst is $71,371 per year in the United States. That figure includes a base salary of $66,424 per year plus an average bonus of $4,947 per year.

Future Outlook

The Bureau of Labor Statistics (BLS) includes social media intelligence analysts in the general category of market research analysts. The BLS estimates that employment of market research analysts is projected to grow by 19 percent through 2031—a much faster growth rate than the average for all occupations. The BLS reports that there are about one hundred thousand openings for market research analysts projected each year, on average, until 2031.

Find Out More

The Beginner's Guide to Social Media Intelligence
www.liferaftinc.com/blog/the-beginners-guide-to-social-media-intelligence
A page within the Life Raft website, this online guide provides an overview of social media intelligence that is ideal for students. It discusses the many uses of social media intelligence and how they relate to various types of social media platforms, including forums, blogs, and microblogging platforms.

National Center for Women & Information Technology
https://ncwit.org
The National Center for Women & Information Technology is a nonprofit organization that works with public and private organizations to increase girls' and women's participation in technology and computing. The center helps organizations with computing staffing needs to recruit, retain, and advance women by providing support, evidence, and action.

The Social Intelligence Lab
https://thesilab.com
The Social Intelligence Lab is an online community for the people who run social listening and intelligence programs. The website includes dozens of free articles and videos about various aspects of social media intelligence.

Source Notes

Introduction: A Popular Activity Generates Jobs

1. Harshal Karanpuriya, "Think Outside the Box: How AI Can Revolutionize Your Social Media Strategy!," LinkedIn, August 3, 2023. www.linkedin.com.

Content Creator

2. Mandy Ison, interview with the author, August 5, 2023.
3. Courtney Park, "A Day in the Life of Content Creator Courtney Park," Microsoft 365, April 5, 2023. https://create.microsoft.com.
4. Joanna Hawley-McBride, "A Day in My Life as a Full-Time Content Creator," Jojotastic, May 5, 2022. https://jojotastic.com.
5. Quoted in Mark Sullivan, "Demand for Content Creators Soars, but Salaries Lag Behind," WeWork, April 26, 2018. www.wework.com.

Social Media Influencer

6. Statista, "Influencer Advertising—United States," 2023. www.statista.com.
7. Quoted in Jessica Booth, "What It's Really like to Be an Instagram Influencer," The List, October 15, 2020. www.thelist.com.
8. Quoted in Booth, What It's Really like to Be an Instagram Influencer."
9. Quoted in Susannah Hutcheson, "How I Became a Makeup Mogul: Beauty Influencer Huda Kattan Talks About Business, Life," USA Today, August 21, 2018. www.usatoday.com.

Artificial Intelligence Data Scientist

10. Quoted in Amit Raja Naik, "A Day in the Life of a Data Scientist: Impacting People's Lives Through the Power of AI ," AIM, April 1, 2022. https://analyticsindiamag.com.
11. Eshna Verma, "A Day in the Life of a Data Scientist," Simplilearn, August 8, 2023. www.simplilearn.com.
12. Quoted in Berkeley School of Information, "What Is Data Science?," January 14, 2021. https://ischoolonline.berkeley.edu.

Social Media Manager

13. Mitra Mehvar, "A Day in the Life of a Social Media Manager: How to Spend Time on Social Media in 2023," Buffer, March 27, 2023. https://buffer.com.
14. Mehvar, "A Day in the Life of a Social Media Manager."
15. Quoted in Stukent, "A Day in the Life of a Social Media Manager," August 30, 2022. www.stukent.com.
16. Quoted in RSK, "A Day in the Life of a Social Media Manager at RSK Group," April 13, 2023. https://rskgroup.com.

Mobile App Developer

17. Harshal Karanpuriya, "Step-by-Step Guide for Mobile App Development," LinkedIn, June 8, 2023. www.linkedin.com.
18. Ahmed Joni, "A Day in the Life of an App Developer," LinkedIn, June 6, 2022. www.linkedin.com.
19. Quoted in Apadmi Careers, "A Day in the Life of an App Developer," Apadmi, March 4, 2021. www.apadmi.com.
20. Dina Destreza, "What Is the Scope for Mobile Apps Company?," Quora, 2022. www.quora.com.
21. Quoted in ReachMobi, "A Day in the Life of an Android Developer [Interview]," September 9, 2019. https://reachmobi.com.
22. Ronald Renaud, "What Is the Future of a Mobile App Developer?," Quora, July 29, 2022. www.quora.com.

Social Media Intelligence Analyst

23. Quoted in Ronnie Gomez, "Social Media Careers: The Skills You Need, Where to Look and Jobs to Consider," Sprout Social, July 7, 2022. https://sproutsocial.com.
24. We Make Heart, "Why Your Brand Should Be Social Listening," LinkedIn, August 1, 2023. www.linkedin.com.
25. Jessica Hammerstein, "A Day in the Life of a Social Media Analyst," Ignite Social Media, March 31, 2023. www.ignitesocialmedia.com.
26. Hammerstein, "A Day in the Life of a Social Media Analyst."
27. Ronnie Gomez, "Social Media Careers."

Interview with a Social Media Manager

Lauren Thomas is an award-winning social media strategist for billion-dollar brands. She has more than twelve years of experience working with Fortune 500 companies, including Macy's, The Coca-Cola Company, and AT&T. She is currently a senior communications manager at Intuit TurboTax, based in San Diego, California. She answered questions about her career by email.

Q: Why did you become a social media manager?
A: I graduated from college before social media emerged as a viable career path. I earned a bachelor's degree in English and decided to pursue a career in marketing. I landed a job at a global advertising and marketing agency and noticed that the marketing landscape was starting to shift from traditional advertising channels, like television commercials and billboards, to social media. I took a leap of faith and joined a startup agency that specialized in social media and influencer marketing. After my time there, I worked at several digital marketing agencies before transitioning to work in-house at Fortune 500 companies. I gravitated to this career—and have stayed in the field for over a decade—because I enjoy working at the intersection of creativity, communication, and pop culture.

Q: Can you describe your typical workday?
A: My typical workdays consist of a lot of meetings! I connect with my team to share status updates and align on priorities. I brainstorm content ideas with my team, review content, and provide feedback. I meet with agency partners and vendors to provide

feedback on campaigns and review performance. I share status updates with senior leadership within my company to keep them informed about campaign launches and ongoing performance.

Some of my meetings require a lot of preparation, so I spend a lot of time preparing and polishing presentations.

Between meetings, I catch up on emails and Slack messages. I also block time to tackle administrative tasks like creating purchase orders and managing budgets.

When we're in campaign production mode, I travel for video shoots and spend the day on set or on location sharing real-time feedback with our talent and agency partners.

I wind down with happy hour or dinner with my team at least once per quarter.

Q: What do you like most about your job?
A: I love that my job gives me the opportunity to be creative and innovative. Social media is constantly evolving so I have to stay on top of trends and changes. I flex my creativity by finding engaging ways to tap into pop culture and channel trends to communicate key brand messages. I flex my innovation by testing and learning as new features and platforms emerge.

I also appreciate that my career has opened the door to so many adventures and opportunities to take big swings. I've spoken at conferences around the country, produced viral videos, worked with celebrity talent, extended Super Bowl campaigns into social media, and achieved a Guinness World Records title for the longest non-TV promotional commercial.

Q: What do you like least about your job?
A: There are a lot of moving parts to navigate when it comes to managing social media for Fortune 500 companies. One of the more challenging elements of my job involves getting alignment and approval from key stakeholders to move projects forward. That ranges from getting legal feedback and approval on content to getting budget approval from senior leadership.

Q: What personal qualities do you find most valuable for this type of work?
A: Content creation for major brands is a team sport! A collaborative approach will enable you to partner with cross-functional teams to move work forward. Creativity will unlock your ability to develop engaging content and campaigns. Curiosity will help you to stay on top of news and trends—online and offline. Attention to detail will enable you to deliver polished work. An analytical mindset will empower you to understand how your content is performing and to optimize your approach to drive better business results.

Q: What advice do you have for students who might be interested in this career?
A: If you're interested in a career in social media, dive in! Get hands-on experience by creating content for your personal brand. Reach out to people who work in the industry and set up informational interviews to learn more about their career journeys. Read trade publications like *Adweek* and *Ad Age* to stay on top of the news and trends in the brand marketing space. Embrace the learning curve. Creating content for your personal brand can be a great entry point into a career in social media. However, there's a big difference between creating content for yourself and creating content on behalf of a brand. Stay open to feedback as you're learning the ropes and growing in your career.

Other Jobs in Social Media

Blogger
Brand manager
Chat specialist
Content strategist
Creative director
Data analyst
Digital communications manager
Digital marketer
Digital project manager
Digital strategist
Interactive producer
Internet marketer
Marketing associate
Multimedia animator
Multimedia artist
Pay per click manager
SEO analyst
SEO strategist
Social media community manager
Social media coordinator
Social media specialist
Telecommunication specialist
User interface designer
Web designer
Webmaster
Website administrator

Editor's note: The online *Occupational Outlook Handbook* of the US Department of Labor's Bureau of Labor Statistics is an excellent source of information on jobs in hundreds of career fields, including many of those listed here. The *Occupational Outlook Handbook* may be accessed online at www.bls.gov/ooh.

Index

Note: Boldface page numbers indicate illustrations.

advertising, 4
  influencer, spending on, 14–15
algorithms, 5
American Marketing Association, 13, 35
App Developers Alliance, 44
App Quality Alliance (AQuA), 44
artificial intelligence (AI), 5
Artificial Intelligence Board of America, 26
artificial intelligence data scientist
  education/training requirements, 22, 25–26
  employers of, 27
  future job outlook, 22, 28
  information on, 28
  number of jobs, 22
  role of, 22–24
  salary/earnings, 22, 27
  skills/personal qualities, 22, 26–27
  typical workday, 24–25
  working conditions, 27
  work settings, 22

Association of National Advertisers (ANA), 36
Association of Software Professionals (ASP), 44

Barker, Emily-Sian, 33
Beginner's Guide to Social Media Intelligence, The, 52
Benton, Brian, 13
Bureau of Labor Statistics (BLS), 58
  on data scientist, 28
  on growth in computer/information technology occupations, 6
  on market research analyst, 51–52
  on software developers, 43

Charnas, Arielle, 18
Charrière, Camille, 16
Chia, Hou, 39
cloud platforms, 26, 40
CMO Council, 5
content creator
  education/training requirements, 7, 11
  employers of, 12
  future job outlook, 7, 13
  information on, 13

number of jobs, 7
role of, 7–9
salary/earnings, 7, 12
skills/personal qualities, 7, 11
typical workday, 9–10
working conditions, 11–12
work settings, 7
Coursera (online tech company), 26, 40

data
marketing and analysis of, 5
structured *vs.* unstructured, 23
Data Science Central (website), 28
Destreza, Dina, 39–40

Gomez, Ronnie, 49–50
Google Data Analytics Professional Certificate, 31

Hammerstein, Jessica, 46, 47–48, 50
Hawley-McBride, Joanna, 10
How to Start a YouTube Channel, 20–21
humanities, benefits of education in, 39

Influencer Podcast, The, 21
Ison, Mandy, 8

Jan, Vilma Un, 42
Joni, Ahmed, 37–38

Kaggle, 28
Karanpuriya, Harshal, 4, 37
Kassandra, Royale, 42
Kay, Heather, 38–39
King, Anthony, 33, 35

Mehvar, Mitra, 30
Meta React Native Specialization Certificate, 40
Meta Social Media Marketing Professional Certificate, 31
microblogs, 5
mobile app developer, **41**
education/training requirements, 37, 39–40
employers of, 43
future job outlook, 37, 43
information on, 44
number of jobs, 37
role of, 37–38
salary/earnings, 37, 43
skills/personal qualities, 37, 40–42
typical workday, 38–39
working conditions, 42
work settings, 37

National Center for Women & Information Technology, 52

Occupational Outlook Handbook (Bureau of Labor Statistics), 58
O'Hagan, Kate, 45, 47

Park, Courtney, 9
PayScale (employment website), 34
Pew Research Center, 4
Pexels (website), 13
ProductionCrate (website), 13, 21

Rich, Kiersten, 19
Risley, Kyle, 31
Rival IQ (social media analytics firm), 34

Sayyad, Sadaf, 24, 25
Social Intelligence Lab, The, 52
social media
 amount of time spent on, 4
 number of active users of, 22
 other jobs in, 58
Social Media Club, 36
social media influencer, 9, **18**
 education/training requirements, 14, 16–17
 employers of, 19–20
 future job outlook, 14, 20
 information on, 20–21
 number of jobs, 14
 role of, 14–15
 salary/earnings, 14, 20
 skills/personal qualities, 14, 17–18
 typical workday, 15–16
 working conditions, 18–19
 work settings, 14
social media intelligence analyst, **49**
 education/training requirements, 45, 48–49
 employers of, 51
 future job outlook, 45, 51–52
 information on, 52
 number of jobs, 45
 role of, 45–47
 salary/earnings, 45, 51
 skills/personal qualities, 45, 49–51
 typical workday, 47–48
 working conditions, 51
 work settings, 45
social media manager, **32**
 education/training requirements, 29, 30–32
 employers of, 34–35
 future job outlook, 29, 35
 information on, 35–36
 interview with, 55–57
 number of jobs, 29
 role of, 29
 salary/earnings, 29, 34–35

skills/personal qualities, 29, 32–33
typical workday, 29–30
working conditions, 33–34
work settings, 29
Social Media Professional Association, 36
Social Media Today, 36
Statista Market Insights (data/business intelligence firm), 4, 14, 15
structured data, 23

Thomas, Lauren, 55
Tobin, James M., 26

University of Texas at El Paso, 13

Vanderbilt University, 40
Verma, Eshna, 24–25

Warakomski, Caitlyn, 15
We Make Heart (digital marketing firm), 46
Women in Data Science (WiDS), 28

Zippia (employment website), 11, 12
ZipRecruiter (employment website), 12, 20

Picture Credits

Cover: mojo cp/Shutterstock

18: Aruta Images/Shutterstock
32: Hiraman/iStock
41: gorodenkoff/iStock
49: gorodenkoff/Shutterstock

About the Author

Bradley Steffens is a novelist, poet, and award-winning author of more than seventy nonfiction books for children and young adults.